Yellow Umbrella Books are published by Capstone Press
151 Good Counsel Drive, P.O. Box 669, Mankato, Minnesota 56002
www.capstonepress.com

Library of Congress Cataloging-in-Publication Data
Cipriano, Jeri S.
    Celebrations / by Jeri Cipriano.
    p. cm.
    Summary: Simple text and photographs introduce holidays that are observed in different countries, such as the celebration of the moon in Vietnam and the celebration of Kwanzaa in the United States.
    ISBN 0-7368-2925-3 (hardcover)—ISBN 0-7368-2884-2 (softcover)
    1. Holidays—Juvenile literature. [1. Holidays.] I. Title.
GT3933.C57 2004
394.26—dc21   2003010970

Editorial Credits
Editorial Director: Mary Lindeen
Editor: Jennifer VanVoorst
Photo Researcher: Scott Thoms
Developer: Raindrop Publishing

Photo Credits
Cover: Charles & Josette Lenars/Corbis; Title Page: Kelly-Mooney Photography/Corbis; Page 2: Lindsay Hebberd/Corbis; Page 3: Reuters NewMedia Inc./Corbis; Page 4: Photodisc; Page 5: AFP/Corbis; Page 6: Comstock; Page 7: Corbis; Page 8: Corel; Page 9: Corel; Page 10: Corel; Page 11: Francoise de Mulder/Corbis; Page 12: Robert Landau/ Corbis; Page 13: Markow Tatiana/Corbis Sygma; Page 14: Craig Lovell/Corbis; Page 15: Corel; Page 16: Creatas/Creatas

1 2 3 4 5 6 09 08 07 06 05 04

Celebrations

by Jeri Cipriano

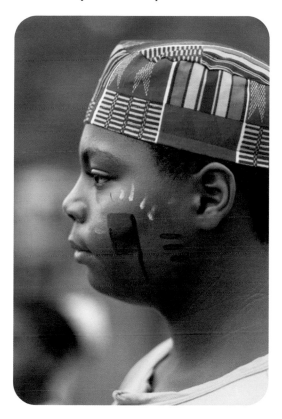

Consultant: Dwight Herold, EdD, Past President,
Iowa Council for the Social Studies

Yellow Umbrella Books

an imprint of Capstone Press
Mankato, Minnesota

Fall

In the fall, West Indians celebrate Carnival. People wear costumes. They march in parades.

2

Vietnamese people celebrate the moon. Children eat moon cakes and carry glowing lanterns.

It is Thanksgiving Day in America. People eat a special meal. They give thanks for things that grow.

In India, people celebrate Diwali. They give each other gifts. They light candles.

Winter

In the winter, people in America celebrate Kwanzaa. They celebrate their African background.

Jewish families all over the world celebrate Hanukkah. They light candles to celebrate freedom.

Chinese people celebrate the
Chinese New Year. People do the
lion dance. They watch a parade.

It is Mardi Gras time in the Philippines. People wear masks. They dance in the streets.

Spring

May Day marks the beginning of spring in many countries. Children dance around a maypole.

Cambodians celebrate the New Year in spring. People dance and throw flower petals.

Cinco de Mayo is a Mexican
celebration. Bands play music.
Dancers wear colorful costumes.

It is Children's Day in Japan.
Families fly fish kites.

Summer

In the summer, Native Americans celebrate their background. They dance the hoop dance.

In July, Americans celebrate Independence Day. Independence Day is America's birthday.

What special days do you celebrate?

Words to Know/Index

background—the way of life of a person's relatives from long ago; pages 6, 14

costume—clothes worn by people during a traditional celebration or holiday; pages 2, 12

maypole—a pole decorated with ribbons and flowers; people dance around maypoles to celebrate May Day; page 10

parade—a line of people, bands, cars, and floats that travels through a town; parades celebrate special events and holidays; pages 2, 8

Word Count: 199
Early-Intervention Level: 16